# RELATIONSHIP CALLING™
## FOR
# BANKERS

## JOHN J. GEHEGAN

ISBN: 0989227707
ISBN-13: 9780989227704
Library of Congress Control Number: 2013908717
Gehegan Associates, San Diego, CA

# DEDICATION

*To Maureen, Brigid, Margaret and John, thanks so much for all the joy and happiness you have brought into my life. When I grow up I want to be just like you.*

# ACKNOWLEDGEMENTS

There are many people to THANK and acknowledge for their support and assistance throughout my career. However, I would like to extend a special note of appreciation to the following:

Angela - My business would not have been possible without your initial support, encouragement and faith in my abilities. Thanks for allowing me to create my dream job and for being a terrific mother to our four children.

Chris Lovett - I could not have asked for a more loyal and dedicated business partner. Your professionalism, integrity and presentation skills are unsurpassed. You have been instrumental in taking this business to new heights. Thanks for taking a risk and believing in my vision.

Ann marie Houghtailing – This book would still be on my to do list without your organization and dedication. Your unique skills allow you to master a number of projects simultaneously. Thanks for your creativity and insight in helping me put into words all of the concepts and ideas I teach.

To all my clients and all the bankers that I have trained, thanks so much for your confidence in my abilities and giving me the opportunity to work with you. Without you none of this would have ever transpired.

# INTRODUCTION

BEGAN MY SELLING CAREER AS a commission – only salesperson. If I didn't sell anything I didn't get paid. Rest assured that everything I teach comes from direct experience and my own collection of mistakes and successes. I was fortunate to have had an excellent sales manager who worked tirelessly to make each of us the best we could be. He never just told us how to do it; he would lead by example and make phone calls with us - a quality I always admired and respected. I have worked side by side with many very successful salespeople. These role models were instrumental to my success and contributed an invaluable education that I've been able to build upon. My depth and breadth of experience has allowed me to address all of the challenges bankers face everyday.

I started my own sales training business in 1983. My objective at the time was to design and deliver customized sales training based on the basic tenets of the sales process. My initial target market was office product companies; an industry I had worked in both as a salesperson and sales manager.

I have always been very conscious of the fact that sales skills and product knowledge are useless without an audience.

Whenever I designed a program for a client I always placed a heavy emphasis on effectively using the telephone to obtain appointments with prospective clients. I would allocate an hour in each of my workshops to allow the participants to make actual "live calls" to prospects with the objective of securing an appointment. I knew if I could get the participants comfortable with using the phone for appointments, all of the other skills we worked on in the workshop would now have an opportunity to be enhanced.

In 1985 I made a cold call to Bill Wofford, an Executive Vice President at Union Bank in Los Angeles, California. Although I had no banking experience I knew Union Bank had a business development team and thought they would be a good prospect for my training. I was successful in convincing Mr. Wofford to give me an appointment. As fate would have it, the bank was going through a transition and eliminating the business development officers. They wanted the account executives that had portfolio responsibility to become better at the sales process. They gave me the opportunity to design and deliver a sales training program for all of their account executives. As part of my due diligence I prepared a questionnaire to learn more about their industry. One of the questions was "What sales skills would you like to improve during this training?"

The constant thread throughout the majority of the responses was to improve their appointment setting skills. I was excited to see this since I had already planned to include the live calling module as part of the training.

Although most of the account executives were apprehensive about making calls in front of their peers, once they saw they could get an appointment they embraced the process.

About six months later I received a call from Ed James, an Executive Vice President at Mitsui Manufacturers Bank. He said that one of his bankers had attended my training at Union Bank and thought the live calling portion of the training was the most valuable training he had received. We had a meeting and he asked me if I could design a training course that would just focus on getting appointments because he felt that this was a skill his bankers needed to improve.

Upon completing this engagement, I saw an opportunity to help bankers become more proficient at using the phone as a business development tool. I changed my focus from delivering customized sales training to creating a one-day Telephone Skills Workshop and began to exclusively target the banking industry. As I learned more about the banking industry I also saw a need to increase the competency of the platform officers who were making calls to their existing customer base and thus I developed my Relationship Calling™ Workshop.

The outbound-calling training I've developed for the banking industry is based on some very simple principles that when applied on a consistent basis will deliver exceptional results. I'm a fan of real world; practical training that bankers can use the very same day. My goal is very simple: to make you better at the one skill that matters most in the sales process – PROSPECTING.

Over the years, I have had the pleasure of working with money center banks, large regional banks and community banks.  I have trained Branch Mangers, Business Bankers, Commercial Banking Officers, Personal Bankers and Licensed Bankers.

I believe that training can be exceptional and still remain accessible. Complicated, convoluted and theoretical concepts don't deliver better results. Great training need not be difficult to integrate; and in fact, is more likely to be embraced and sustained if it's easy to navigate.

Although many of the tenets I discuss are applicable across all sales organizations, there is uniqueness to the banking industry.  This book is written for any banker who needs to acquire new business or broaden and deepen existing relationships. This book captures the essence of the concepts we teach in our training.  We focus on a simple process – SELL THE APPOINTMENT.

I have divided the book into three sections:  The **Relationship Calling**™ section focuses on contacting existing clients. The **Business Calling** Section focuses on contacting prospective clients.  The **Managing the Process** section is designed to help managers maximize the performance of each banker's outbound calling activity.

# RELATIONSHIP CALLING™

**S**ales training and product knowledge training fails to address prospecting. It's important that you're well trained on sales skills and generally most banks do an excellent job of training you on the basic tenets of the sales process. In addition, banks typically provide good training on their products and services. All of this is valuable. The only problem is that none of this training addresses the task of getting someone in front of you. This is because most sales training and product knowledge training is developed with the assumption that you already have a client in front of you.

The features and benefits of a product, together with an understanding of the sales process, are necessary information, but they won't help you to reach your sales goals. Reaching goals requires bankers to engage in an activity that most bankers struggle with because they have not been trained on how to do it effectively.

If you have felt lost or inadequate when it comes to prospecting, it's simply that no one has shown you *how*. Someone has probably told you what to do, "Call these customers," or "Open fifteen checking accounts this month." *What* to do is not generally the problem. The struggle is *how* do you do it? The practical nature of my training is focused exclusively on the *how*. I'm dedicated to those on the frontlines who are required to increase revenue and build relationships.

**Prospecting is the most critical component of the sales process.** While many sales experts and gurus contend that closing is the most important step in the sales process, I challenge this long held belief in particular when it comes to banking. As I mentioned earlier, the hardest part of the sales process is getting someone in front of you – period. Once you have a customer in front of you, you're able to engage them, understand what they need, and make the appropriate recommendations; but without an audience, you've got no opportunity to sell anything to anyone. I can't count the number of bankers who say, "I love working with customers." "However, it's hard to get them to come into the bank."

There's a very good reason customers don't come into the bank anymore. The bank has trained them to stay out of the branch. With everything from direct deposit to online banking and now mobile banking, the bank has built a structure that effectively limits reasons to step foot into the branch. The banking industry has continued to devise tools and solutions that prevent the need for interaction.

Now, it's as if the entire banking system has looked up and noticed that it's really hard to sell when you don't have any customers in front of you. Traffic is down and your goals are rising. If you don't master prospecting what are you going to do?

When was the last time Miss Cardillo came in with a busload of her bingo pals to open checking accounts? Probably never, so you need to reach out to your customers and present compelling reasons for them to engage with you. The fact that they have their money sitting in your bank is a great start.

Bankers are generally hired because they are competent and skilled about servicing a customer's needs. As a trainer, I can tell you that the vast majority of bankers know what they're doing. I've never taught one banker a single thing about banking. I know that servicing your customer is the best and most satisfying part of your job. I want to make sure that you have a steady stream of customers to serve.

**Effective prospecting cures all other potential inadequacies in the sales process**. The more customers you have in front of you, the more opportunities you have to sell, and the more opportunities you have to sell, the more you are able to perfect the sales process.

There isn't a single activity in the world that is not improved through the discipline of repetition; since prospecting is the most valuable step in the sales process, once you've mastered this activity, you've conquered the process. Success ultimately equals more success.

**Using the phone as a business development tool isn't only effective; it's economical.** Picking up the phone remains the most economical activity to building a business. While marketing and advertising create awareness, they rarely drive traffic or increase engagement. A slick, expensive marketing campaign doesn't replace prospecting. Advertising can be used to great effect to enhance branding efforts, but at the end of the day it's the relationship that a customer develops with a banker that will increase revenue and reduce attrition.  Marketing campaigns don't create customers; they create impressions. Loyal customers are created through experience. When you call and advocate for your customer, you're providing an experience that transcends brochures, billboards, and commercials.

There's also a larger organizational financial benefit. The sooner and better a banker is trained, the more revenue she will generate, and the more likely she'll be to enjoy her work and want to remain with the bank. No one wants to stay in an environment where they don't feel successful or supported. Training people mitigates turnover and increases job satisfaction.

By and large people really want to perform well, but it can be a challenge if they aren't properly trained or simply don't possess the skills for success.

**Contacting your customers is more critical than ever before.** Technology has created incredible convenience and the ability to bank anywhere at anytime. This convenience has also created distance. Customers are able to jump from one bank to another without the slightest thought because in their minds they aren't leaving a relationship; they're just leaving an institution. Between call centers that may be on the other side of the globe and technology that allows me to avoid contact with the bank up my street, infusing your bank with humanity is more important than it's ever been.

The technological race and pressure to produce newer and innovative ways of delivering service will not wane. It's remarkable and exciting and it's presented an unexpected challenge or more accurately – opportunity. Rather than being a victim of technology, bankers need to see their personal connection to the customer as even more important, even more valued, and therefore requiring even greater attention and protection.

**Bankers don't sell, do they?** If you were hired as a banker and someone has handed you a phone and a call list, you may be feeling duped. It's quite possible that no one mentioned the word quota or goal to you in your job interview.

You might have been under the impression that as a banker you'd be sitting in a nice upholstered chair waiting for customers to come to your desk and ask you questions about how they could sign up for more fabulous products. As it turns out, you were wrong. It's okay. A lot of bankers started their career with that same fantasy.

As it so happens, banking, like the vast majority of jobs in the United States, require selling something to someone. The great news is that you already work for a great company, so your job is going to be much easier than you imagine. But it will require you to learn a few things. Not to worry. I'm going to start by redefining your perception of selling and teaching you how to make this entire process of picking up the phone a much easier task.

**Sell the appointment, not the product.** In part, the reason (why) prospecting is so loathed, is that everyone assumes that they're supposed to be hocking this week's product special on the phone. You're not. Selling product over the phone is a losing proposition and creates an unnecessary pressure for the banker. It's a short-term transactional strategy in direct opposition to my Relationship Calling™, which favors servicing the client.

Even if you have a great product, I as your customer might not need it; in which case, I don't care. Focus on how you can help me and what I need, not what you've got to sell today.

Transactions are short and might help you to fill a goal, but relationships are long-lived and help you to build a business. Over the years, I have built many long-term relationships with my clients. On many occasions clients will ask me to participate in a conference call or attend a meeting. They always ask me what my fee would be to participate and my answer is always the same. NO CHARGE. I tell them I am not in the fee business. My goal is and always will be to grow and maintain relationships with my clients. If you put your client's needs first, your goals will be realized and your clients will always see you as a resource, rather than a transactional salesperson.

If you invite your customer to come into the bank with the goal of saving or making them a bit more money then they see the value in meeting with you. The meeting is about discovery, not product pushing, and the agenda is set around what's best for your customer, not checking a box for your quota. If you build a strategy based on what is best for your customer and you prospect consistently, the goals will be taken care of on their own.

In addition to supporting your goals, getting clients in front of you serves other purposes. In an age of hypersensitivity to identify theft and scams, it just makes sense to have your customer come into the bank and interact with you directly. Meeting your client in person builds customer confidence and loyalty.

**I'm not a Salesperson**. This simple sentence has been uttered by bankers, lawyers, dentists, engineers, accountants, and countless other professionals. If you're under the impression that you're not a salesperson, you're in great company. I'll let you in on a secret. All professional service providers are salespeople. Without the ability to sell to clients, their business could not exist. When someone pays for your service, you've sold something.

The persistent resistance towards selling has caused unnecessary grief to a lot of people, but in fact selling is how all business functions. If you can change some of your ideas about selling, you can have an incredible impact. Your relationship to selling is directly related to your performance. In all of the years I've trained people I can tell you that no one comes to my training excited, energized and overjoyed to pick up the phone. The vast majority of bankers who attend our training do so under duress.

Most were "voluntold" to come to the training. It just doesn't happen. Some participants have spent some time before training strategizing on how to get OUT of training. I never take this personally. After all, it can't really be me; they haven't even met me yet. Many people develop this anxiety because they think our training is "telemarketing " and they now see themselves as that guy who calls during dinner hawking long distance phone plans or magazine subscriptions.

Once they see the value of reaching out to their customers in a professional manner, a total metamorphous occurs. When they see that the overwhelming majority of customers are cordial to them, their perception about calling changes.  Countless participants will come up to me after the class and tell me how they dreaded coming to this class and now are so glad they came.  I believe the main reason for this turnaround is that they now see themselves as an advocate for the customer, not some product pusher.

Despite what you imagined or what you were told, you are expected to increase revenue for the bank. It is a critical part of your role as a banker, but this isn't just about your bank. This is about you. If you can learn to create more opportunity and generate more revenue for the bank, you'll create more opportunity for yourself. Prospecting is a highly valued skill that is critical in every economic climate.  Regardless of the institution or the status of the economy, everyone wants someone who is skilled at prospecting.

With an open mind, a positive attitude, and a little discipline, you can be extremely successful. How do I know this? In the past thirty years, along with my associates, helping bankers to be successful has been our entire mission. We have trained tens of thousands of bankers to perfect just one skill – prospecting. Our track record assures me that I can train any willing banker to meet his or her goals with relative ease.

Every banker has goals. This is the nature of your industry. And with goals comes someone whose goal is for you to make your goals! You see where this is all leading? You probably have someone asking you weekly, if not daily *"How many calls have you made?" "How many appointments did you get?" "How many accounts have you opened?"* This pressure can cause a lot of anxiety for bankers. In fact, for many bankers it's the most stressful part of their job. The solution is to make goal! I am invested and committed to your success because I am all too familiar with the anxiety and frustration that prospecting causes.

When I first started selling I was terrible on the phone! I can distinctly remember making a call to an attorney and as I was talking he hung the phone up on me. Guess what?   I continued talking into the phone all the while listening to dial tone because I did not want the salesperson next to me to know that I had just got blown out. I feared the phone because it was impersonal. I was much better in a face-to-face environment because I could use my personality and it was harder for them to immediately get rid of me. However, I soon realized I needed to get better on the phone because it was more efficient and a better use of my time. I attended a weeklong training program on sales skills for Lanier business products in Atlanta, Georgia. The instructor began the class by asking us what part of the sales process we found to be the most challenging. I immediately responded that I wanted to improve my phone skills. We did some role - playing and watched videos on what to do and what not to do when making calls. They provided me with a scripting tool to use when making calls. This became my elixir. I went back to my office in Los Angeles and started making calls using the script almost word-for-word, and it worked. My anxiety waned and my confidence increased. And as my confidence increased my sales grew and my income increased dramatically.

**"I'm not like Bob. Bob is a natural born salesperson."** As a seasoned sales professional, I'm here to tell you that the "natural born salesperson" is a total myth. What does "natural born sales person" even mean? Have you ever heard anyone identify a "natural born structural engineer", a "natural born brain surgeon", or a "natural born mortician"?

I have heard some version of this phrase in relation to sales professionals more times than I can count. This inaccurate, detrimental myth that sharp dressers who can tell a good story can sell anything suggests that selling is the domain of the few, and not everyone can learn to sell more or sell better. This just isn't so. Selling is a skill. Anyone, and yes, I mean anyone, can get better at selling. It's merely a question of priority, discipline, and consistency. If you choose to take a bit of time to learn how to get better, you will be richly rewarded for your efforts.

I once had a young man in my training class who was full of energy and enthusiasm, but admitted he was not very successful at the "art of selling" as he put it. Upon the conclusion of the class he promised to use the tools we provided him and strive to get better at making appointments. Some 15 years later I was making a business development call to an Executive Vice President at a large regional bank. Upon taking my call the first thing he said to me was "I remember you; your training was one of the best things that happened to me in my banking career." Now I don't promise you that you will achieve EVP status at your bank, but I will promise you that with some desire and dedication you will get better at selling. Some people will be better than others at selling; a fact that is true of every skill-based activity from golf to cooking.

While everyone can't be the top salesperson, there's plenty of room to improve, create new opportunities, make more money, and let's not forget – enjoy your job! You are more likely to engage in an activity when you're successful. Let's face it, selling isn't going anywhere, so if you get better at it, you'll feel better about doing it, and everybody wins.

If you've been in banking for most of your career, you have no doubt noted the shift from reactive selling to proactive revenue generation. The times have changed and banking isn't going back, but you can adapt; and I'm going to help you.

**I hate selling.** Welcome to the human race! Most people do not want to identify as a salesperson and nearly everyone hates the idea of selling, despite the fact that we're all selling something to someone. But what if I told you that the reason you hate selling is because no one has ever accurately defined selling or taught you how to prospect effectively? You probably have the idea that selling is about getting people to do something they may not want to do. Selling is not manipulating, coercing, or convincing anyone to do anything.

Selling is really just trying to serve people, but not just anyone, but rather people who need you! Selling is actually important work. Selling the right product to the right customer inspires loyalty, because when we sell well, we save or make our clients money. Selling is never about what the bank needs. Selling is about what the customer needs. I am personally completely turned off by the words, "PROMOTION" and "SPECIAL," and would like the words removed from all prospecting activity. Calling about a PROMOTION or SPECIAL is not a call strategy and more importantly, it doesn't serve your customer. You might think your Credit Card is the finest Credit card on the planet earth, and maybe it is, but if I don't need it, I don't care. Having a SPECIAL is not a compelling reason for customers to speak with you. In order to serve your customers you must reach out to them with the goal of improving their circumstance and not pushing the latest product.

Selling is about understanding who your customer is, what they need, and making recommendations based on those needs. That's it. When your strategy is customer-centric and focused on serving rather than transacting, your entire approach changes.   Guess what else changes? The way you feel about selling changes.

**Calling enhances your sales skills.** When you engage with your client, you become better able to assess their needs, provide solutions and address their concerns.  Using the phone in and of itself is a form of sales training with real life customers in the real world environment.   We learn by doing. Becoming a better sales person is a natural by product of calling.

And as you become more adept at making recommendations, your expertise together with your confidence and competence, increases.  You become a better banker. Imagine that! Calling actually helps you develop professionally and serves you as well as your customer.

**I don't 'like getting sales calls!** We all have an aversion to "sales calls." Any call that interrupts time with my family to separate me from my hard earned money is a call I'm reluctant to take. The calls you're making serve your customers, and when executed professionally, your customers appreciate your call. I can practically see bankers rolling their eyes at this statement. Remember I've been doing this for a long time, and I've got an arsenal of data to support my position. *Professional sales calls* are geared to serve the client.

I was doing a Business Development Workshop training many years ago for a client in Los Angeles and during the live calling portion of the training one of the bankers was calling on a temporary accountant agency in Beverly Hills.  The principal answered the phone and immediately asked the banker if this was some type of sales solicitation. The banker replied that indeed he was making some business development calls.  The principal then replied, "Good. I would like to talk with you. My bank has lost the personal touch." I tell this story many times in my training classes when the subject of sales calls being an annoyance surfaces.

Just imagine, if this banker did not make the call he would have allowed the competition to take away a potential client.

It's easy to come to the prospecting process with a biased point of view, because you may have received these calls yourself or have been making sales calls without proper training, which has influenced your opinion. Remember, you aren't a stranger. You're their banker.  You don't get to decide that your customer doesn't want to speak with you. That's your customer's decision, but if you don't call you're denying your customer access to your service. You're also denying your customer an important opportunity to build a relationship with you.

**If you don't call they think you don't care.** The number one reason a customer leaves a bank is seller indifference. If a bank isn't contacting their customers, their customers have no perceived relationship, and therefore feel invisible and irrelevant. Customers leave because no one knows who they are, and the bank feels like an anonymous entity that has lost sight of their customers. This neglect erodes your customer base and allows your competition to gain market share.

It might surprise you to learn that when you call customers to serve their needs and help them, they appreciate getting your call.

I once taught a class in Little Rock, AR and the participants bombarded me with reasons why people in Little Rock would not appreciate being called. I'm given the same list of reasons in every city I work in – some might call these reasons excuses. One banker called a client who was extremely wealthy and had been with the bank a long time. His response was not irritation that she had called, but confusion that it had taken the bank so long to call. He said, "It's about time you people called me and checked up on me. I was starting to wonder if anyone cared. Yes, I would like to come in and talk to you." This is not unusual.

Bankers make the assumption that if a customer needs something, he'll contact them. A customer may not know what he or she needs and so when you fail to call the customer, you fail the customer. Every customer relies on your knowledge and expertise. That's why they come to you in the first place.

You aren't selling magazine subscriptions or asking for political donations. You're a professional. You're their banker and they've chosen you. Your call is as important as a call from their doctor, lawyer, or accountant. Calling on your customers is *never* about products. Calling your customers is about maintaining and growing an established relationship. When your call is focused on the customer instead of calling about products, you're going to feel better about calling.

It's important to remember that transactions are always about selling, but relationships are always about buying!   Relationships position you as a valued resource. We trust people and relationships--- not product pushers.

**Retention demands attention.** Now that you know that customers leave because no one pays attention, the natural extension of logic is that customers *stay* because someone (you) does.

Customers want to feel valued and well advised. There is no better way to communicate your gratitude for their business and express your concern for their interests than calling.

Personal contact increases retention. What would make you feel more valued, a mass mailer or a personal contact? When you evaluate the options, the choice is clear. We all want to be personally acknowledged, which is why picking up the phone is a retention activity that helps to ensure you maintain the market share that you have earned.

Anonymity erodes customer relations. Connecting directly with your customer and providing high touch, quality service only improves and strengthens loyalty. In addition to being a banker you're a consumer. You have undoubtedly experienced various levels of service and commitment. Don't you want to feel valued and appreciated? We remain with companies that acknowledge our importance. Your customers are no different than you.

**Your competition doesn't want you to call your customer.** You may have noticed that banking is a fiercely competitive industry, with competitors who are spending time and money strategizing about how to increase their market share by taking your customers away from you. If you elect not to call your customer, your competitor will be happy to make that call. Without even realizing it, every time you don't call your customer, you're choosing to deliver that customer to your competitor. When you don't call, you're practically working for the competition by easing their workload.

Because competition isn't going away, neither is calling. The only way to communicate your point of differentiation in the market is by reaching out to your customer. Let's be honest, it's very difficult in the banking business to identify differentiation.  Most bank products are homogenous. Your connection to your customers *is* how you differentiate yourself and make yourself relevant. Products don't differentiate institutions, but rather people are the unique difference.

**You are a valuable asset to your customers.** Do you have value? If you answered yes, and you should answer yes (otherwise you might be in the wrong business), then you are actually depriving your clients of your unique value when you fail to call them. Think about that. How many times has a customer come into the bank while you were busy? They could have worked with someone else, but they didn't. They elected to wait for you. Why? Because you are valuable to them and they want your service and expertise. You're their personal, trusted financial resource and if you don't call your customers you're effectively committing financial malpractice. Most customers don't have the skills necessary to protect and grow their money, which is why they come to you in the first place.

Banks are simply made of people. In a nearly overwhelming sea of banking choices, customers need to feel that they have a relationship with you in order to stay with you. Relationships require contact.

And contact must be driven by you because you're responsible for deepening the relationship, not the customer. The last thing you want is to only have interaction with customers when there's a problem. Crisis should never be the only reason for contact.

There are countless times during our training where a banker will make a call to a client and the client oftentimes will thank the banker for calling. Regardless of whether or not we make an appointment we have created a bond with that customer in that someone from the bank actually cares about them. I can assure you that these customers will never leave the bank due to indifference and when they need something they will call you.

**What if a customer asks me a question and I don't have an answer?** Bankers worry that if they start making calls, a customer might ask them a question they cannot answer. Let me assure you that sometimes a customer will absolutely ask you a question for which you have no answer. However, this will only happen once. Why? Because once that question is asked, you'll make darn sure to have the answer next time. You won't forget the answer the next time you're asked the question.

It's also okay to simply tell someone that you need to get back to them regarding their question. No one expects you to have all of the answers. Don't worry about what you don't know because you're never going to know everything anyway.

Once you think you've learned everything you need to know about a product line, the bank is likely to make changes. Besides you already know more about the bank's products and services than your customer, so if there's something you aren't clear about, your customer will generally understand. The very nature of calling increases your product knowledge. All of the manuals, brochures and product knowledge in the world cannot compete with direct experience. You retain more information through dialogue and repetition than reading a manual. Remember learning how to drive? Reading about driving is nothing like the direct experience of navigating the road, reacting to potential obstacles, and making critical decisions. You cannot become an expert at driving by reading behind a book; you've got to get behind a wheel. Your profession is not different. You become a better banker by serving your clients.

I've taught people who have been in banking for forty years along side those who have been on the job for four days. Guess what? Banking experience rarely determines a person's success with calling. The closer people follow the training, the higher their success rate, and needless to say those who know less tend to follow the training with greater care and attention.

I once taught a class in Indiana with a young woman who had barely gone through orientation and was pretty sure she was simply in the training to observe, and that she did not expect to make any calls herself. I explained that common sense combined with the training would allow her to make calls with everyone else. She tried to bargain and negotiate so that she wouldn't have to make calls, but in the end she made the first appointment of the evening. She was elated. If someone with very little experience can make an appointment then anyone can be successful.

**Transform excuses into action.** There are more excuses not to call customers than there are customers. *These calls never lead to business. I don't even have time to make these calls. I'm not in the mood today; I'll do it tomorrow.* And just like that, you've convinced yourself not to call.

I've heard EVERYTHING including that no one in the state of Tennessee will answer the phone on Wednesday night, because Wednesday night is church night. It turns out that there are plenty of heathens answering their phones, so we make lots of contacts even on a Wednesday night in Tennessee. In Wisconsin I've been told that no one answers the phone during a Green Bay game. Believe it or not people do.

You might say that there's no time, but let me promise you that someone can follow you around and squeeze out forty-five minutes to an hour in your day.  If you make time instead of excuses you're going to be a lot more successful. If you simply make a commitment to call for forty-five minutes to an hour a day and keep that commitment, you can easily meet your goals. Don't try to make one call in the morning, one before lunch, and another in between customers. Why?  Because the hardest call to make is the first call, and if you're making one call at a time sandwiched between other activities, you're making the first call over and over again. If there's something you don't like to do, make the task easier, not harder on yourself. Dispersing calls throughout your day is unquestionably harder.

It's really very simple. If calling is a priority and you commit to your priority, you and your bank will meet and exceed your goals.

What can possibly be more important than deepening your relationship with your customers and creating more opportunity for them?

**Plan your call.** Most people simply do not adequately prepare to make a call to a customer. Too often you are handed a list and you simply start at the top and start dialing without any preparation. A lack of preparation can compromise your success and lead to more discomfort. A little planning goes a long way. I also want to clarify, that I really do mean *a little* planning. It is not necessary to do an in depth analysis before you make a call. A simple and quick review of the customer's relationship will give you all the information you need to set an appointment. It's prudent to save the in depth analysis for the appointment when you meet with your customer face to face.

Pull a list that has enough information that directs you to your goal. Are you looking for customers with maturing CDs, customers who don't have a checking account or may be a candidate for a HELOC?

Once you have selected a list, do a quick customer review and note potential needs this customer may have. This might be a large balance in a savings account or they may have a debit card but no credit card – this will give you an understanding of the existing relationship and allow you to probe for a possible need. You should have two specific products or services that will complement their existing relationship. This will allow you to make meaningful recommendations or reasons to set an appointment. If they aren't interested in Plan A or Plan B, then conclude the call and thank them for their time. You don't want to make a laundry list and come across as a product pusher. Your goal is to set appointments and strengthen relationships. The single best compliment you can get from your customer is that every time you call, you have valuable information that keeps them informed and help them grow or protect their money.

**The value of scripting.** In each of our trainings we design a customized calling guide for the bankers to use when making calls. I am a believer in having a structure when making calls. Many people abhor the idea of using a script because most scripts are written to sound canned and do not allow for flexibility. I believe you can use a script and not have it sound like a script if it is written in a conversational manner.

The script establishes the flow of the call. It allows you to frame how you want the call to proceed and cover the most salient points.

A script should be used as guide. It keeps you on track and helps you remain on topic. Also, having scripted answers to objections is vital in moving the call forward. Keep in mind the caller is only reason any script sounds scripted. Stay focused, conversational and on message.

**How do I begin a call?** Make sure that you have the account holder on the line simply by asking with an inflection, *Good afternoon, I was calling to speak with Mr. Cardillo?* Once you have confirmed that you're speaking to the account holder, begin by introducing yourself and the bank, being sure to identify the branch. We want customers to know that their bank in their town is calling them and not some call center a thousand miles a way.

**Recognize the call as an intrusion.** It takes some retraining, but immediately after introducing yourself on a call, *any* phone call, you should always ask, "Did I catch you at a bad time, or do you have a moment?" You might be asking yourself, "Why would you give someone the opportunity to disengage?" But it's quite the opposite. When you ask permission you elevate your standard of professionalism.   Besides if someone wants to get rid of you they will do so regardless of whether or not you ask.  If you fail to ask for someone's time you are effectively inviting him to cut you off and tell you they aren't interested.  How many times when you receive an inbound call does the caller ask "Do you have a moment?" I will bet it's rare.  So why not use a little common courtesy? When the customer acknowledges that they have a moment you now know they are **LISTENING.**

The fact of the matter is when you ask someone if it's a good time to speak, there are really only three possible responses to the question. "*Yes, this is a good time*"– in which case you will proceed. "*This isn't a great time, but what is this about?*" By inquiring about the nature of the call the customer has now given you permission to proceed. And finally, "*No, this is not a good time.*" in which case you simply need to ask them "When would be a better time to call?"  Knowing the typical responses to this important question allows you to remain in control and move the call forward.

I have found that the vast amount of people will elect to speak with you. Most will be pleasant and if you behave like a professional, they'll treat you like a professional. There's nothing worse than getting thirty or forty seconds into the reason for your call only to be cut off. This single question will alter the course of the call because it allows the customer to permit you to move forward. In truth you have a ten second window to engage your customer, so make sure that you use that time wisely.

By recognizing the call as an interruption and asking for your customer's time you will differentiate yourself from the majority of callers who don't ask.

**Always verify your customer's satisfaction.**  Once you have confirmed that the customer has time to speak with you, it is time to get another green light. So the flow of the call now goes like this: "I have two reasons for calling today.  First, I wanted to make sure we are handling your banking needs to your satisfaction.  Are we meeting your expectations?"  Some people worry that this will open a can of worms, but if they aren't happy with you now then they certainly aren't going to be open to expanding their relationship. If there is an issue that you cannot resolve immediately, do not proceed with your call.  Advise the customer that you will look into the matter and call them back.  Be sure to let the customer know that you will be calling back at a specific date and time.  The onus is now on you to follow up.  Even if you are unable to resolve the issue to their total satisfaction, your customer will remember you and the next time you call you won't just be a voice at the other end of the line.  You'll be the person who followed up and did what they said they were going to do.

**Don't give information before getting it.** When you lead with a product you limit your audience and elevate resistance. Your job is to lower resistance so that you're able to engage in a meaningful dialogue. The best way to lower resistance is to avoid product pitching and focus on asking high quality open-ended questions.  This will allow you to learn more about the customer and determine whether or not you can help them.

Here is an excellent segue into your second reason for calling. "My second reason for calling is that in reviewing your account I noticed that you are not taking advantage of our ….. May I get your answers to a few quick questions to determine if this may have some value for you?" Now you have the opportunity to probe and qualify before spouting off the latest and greatest checking account you have.

**Don't ramble. Get to the point.** There is a tendency to believe that the longer you're on the call, the more successful you are, but success is not measured in duration, but rather in appointments. It's easy to want to meander and ask more questions about someone's dog or trip to Italy all the while forgetting your purpose for calling. Plenty of people will enjoy chatting with you, but will never buy anything from you. This is not success.

Be economical with your dialogue and get to your point quickly. You don't need to go into great depth over the phone – that's what you will do during your appointment.  It's also important to value your customer's time rather than fill it with idle chitchat. Make the call a valuable communication that is appreciated by your customer.

**Ask questions. Don't assume you know the answer.** People will frequently not call a customer because they feel they *know* what the customer will say or want. It's not our job to decide for our customers, but rather to provide solutions.  We can't possibly offer solutions unless we are asking excellent questions. Don't assume that their account at your bank is the only account the customer possesses and don't assume they understand all of their options. When we decide for our customers we limit their options as well as the opportunities for the bank to serve the customer.

I was doing a training program in Minneapolis and we were making calls to customers who had maturing CDs. The objective of the call was to set an appointment for one of the financial advisors to discuss alternative investments.   One of the bankers called a customer who had a $50,000.00 CD. He agreed to make the appointment.  She then asked if he had CDs at other banks and he indicated that he had a number of CDs at other institutions that were not providing much of a return. This was a classic example of calling a customer and by asking an additional question, discovering a great opportunity to assist them.  What if she did not call and allowed one of the other banks to call?

**Talk about the customer, not the bank.** It's easy to talk at the customer about all the great products and services the bank has but the information is only relevant in relationship to the customer. It's important to listen, actively listen, more than you speak. We all want to be heard and validated and listening communicates respect and concern. When you don't listen the customer assumes you don't care.

**Your voice is all you have.** When you call someone, you are stripped of all the visual cues that make you YOU. Your smile, your warmth and that tailored suit have no impact.   And because you don't have anything other than your voice to connect to the person on the other end of the line, your voice is magnified. Tone, pitch, energy and hesitation are amplified in the absence of visual content.

It's important that your voice expresses enthusiasm.  Don't let the phone alter your personality.  Visualize your customer as if they were standing right in front of you.  If you are engaging when interacting directly with someone, you can still be engaging on the phone. The principle is to behave no differently on the phone than you do in person.

I personally try to visualize what the person on the other end of the phone looks like.  This helps me to see them as a person not just a voice on the phone.

You may have heard the expression "smile and dial." When you meet someone in person you typically smile. You should wear that same smile when making calls. Your customer will see and hear your smile.

Don't slouch, speak clearly and try not to speak too quickly. Your posture affects the delivery and tone of your voice. Take your time. Speak a little slower to compensate for the lack of visual communication.

I would highly recommend using a wireless headset when making calls. It will allow you to have your hands free but more importantly it will allow you to stand up and walk around. When you stand up and speak your voice resonates with a greater projection thus producing a higher level of confidence and conviction. Whatever you do not let the phone alter your overall personality and presence.

**Be prepared for resistance**. People say 'No' when they don't *know* what you're offering. The 'no' is reflexive and predictable. If you've never heard 'No', you've never called anyone. This reflexive response doesn't merely occur on a phone call. Think about when you're shopping in a retail store and a salesperson approaches you. How do most people respond when that salesperson asks if they need help, "No, just looking."

This is a reflex 'No'. Once you understand that the response is expected, you can address how to manage the response and create some rules around your process.

If you're going to give up after the first "NO" then do yourself a favor, do your bank a favor and most importantly do your customers a favor --- don't call them.

**Should I ever take 'No' for an answer?** Yes. We don't want you to push past twenty No's and alienate your customer. The goal is not to get someone to hang up on you. However, we know from experience that overcoming objections and addressing customer concerns can increase your conversion rate. So how many times should we respond to an objection? Three times. The answer is three with a caveat. If you find someone's "No" is escalating or constant, you need to end the conversation. I know what you're thinking. How do I respond to these objections? We cover this extensively in our training, but let me just give you a few examples of the most common objections with some possible responses.

*"**I'm not interested**"*. This is in fact the most common objection and is generally uttered before you even explain why you're calling. Most bankers simply accept this "Reflexive NO" and say something like, "Well call me if you ever need anything." This response is weak and lacks conviction. A more productive response is, *"I can understand that you wouldn't be interested in something we haven't fully had the opportunity to explore. My only purpose for calling you today was to see if we might help you make your banking more convenient and possibly earn you a bit more money. When will you be in the branch again so we can discuss this further?"*

*"**I need to speak with my spouse**"*. This objection typically occurs after you have opened a dialogue and some interest has been generated. After all why would they want to speak to their spouse if they were not interested? Instead of telling them to call you back after they speak with your spouse, try to get an incremental commitment. *"I can appreciate that you need to speak with your husband/wife. Based on what we've discussed does this sound as if it might be of value to your spouse?*

*Can we set up an appointment for both you and your wife to meet here at the branch?" Does next Thursday later in the day work for you and your wife?"*

There really are only a handful of common, regular objections you'll receive. Nothing works 100% of the time. However, if you learn how to respond to these objections rather than quit, you will mitigate lost opportunities and experience a higher conversion rate.

Keep in mind that your tone matters as well. Be respectful and professional, never confrontational or terse. Your goal is to lower resistance and invite further discussion. If you prepare for objections, you will not be surprised by them, and you'll feel better about knowing when and how to push past them.

**What if my customer is happy at another bank?** While your client is statistically likely to have accounts at various institutions, you shouldn't be deterred by this fact. I like to remind bankers that the only two buyers that exist in all sales environments are users and non-users; they are either using a product or service or they aren't. Which buyer is easier to sell to? The user, because they have bought off on the concept and have realized a benefit. Suppose you're calling on a maturing CD list for the purpose of getting an appointment for the financial advisor. Would you rather hear the customer tell you that they have an advisor or have them say they only want FDIC products? The answer is obvious. You would much prefer to have the person that has the advisor since they have bought off on the concept. Have you ever tried to sell a HELOC to someone who doesn't understand a HELOC? It's much harder because you are starting from zero, but if someone already has a HELOC they might want to know if there's a better opportunity for them.

There's no reason to be intimidated by someone who banks elsewhere or has a similar product. It's merely an adjustment of perception that allows you to engage in a professional dialogue and ascertain how you might be of service. So much about calling is about your perception. If you perceive competition as an impenetrable threat that shuts you down, then your opportunities are greatly limited. However, if you see competition as a qualifying tool, it's not a detriment that a customer already has a relationship with a bank. It's important that you never trash or criticize your competition, but instead simply present what you have to offer, thereby giving your customer an option. There may be real value and an advantage to explore alternatives. It's your responsibility to share those options with your client. Providing a comparison merely positions you as your customer's advocate. Wouldn't you want someone looking out for you? When appropriately presented, your customer values your support in helping to make informed financial decisions. Furthermore, we aren't asking the customer to move their entire relationship based on a phone call.

**It's not about you. Don't take rejection personally.** The primary reason that people fear calling is rejection. No one enjoys being rejected. The truth is when you behave like a telemarketer you get treated like a telemarketer, which is why it is so very important to learn how to call clients like a banker. When you learn how to call on relationships rather than about products, most of your customers don't reject you. Most of the time the way you behave dictates how you'll be treated.

Of the more than 75,000 people we've trained, we have found that the person you call will actually be rude or hang up on you less than 2% of the time. You may question this statistic because 1.) You remember the bad calls and you took it personally or 2.) You haven't been properly trained so you may be behaving more like a telemarketer than a banker.

The great news about rejection is that it gets you closer to the next person who will say "Yes" to you. The most important thing you can do if you get rejected is to pick up the phone immediately and make the next call. Never end your prospecting on a negative note, because that's what you'll remember tomorrow when you have to pick up the phone and start all over again.

It's also important to understand that someone's rudeness towards you isn't at all about you. Before you connect with the person at the other end of the line, there's a whole day that happened before that moment. It's quite possible that day wasn't a great day.

You may be reaching someone who lost a job, or whose roof caved in, or whose dog ran away or all of the above! You're the easiest person to snap at because you're anonymous. When you think about all of these possibilities, it's a whole lot easier not to take rejection personally.

If you start to ponder about some anonymous rude person who might answer the phone, you begin to construct a great list of reasons for why you shouldn't call: *People don't like getting these calls.*

*If a customer wanted something they would call. These calls never lead to business.* And just like that, you've convinced yourself not to call.

I was doing a training program in Santa Rosa, California and we were calling customers who were pre - approved for a home equity line of credit. This young banker called on a customer who immediately went into a profanity laced tirade complaining about how his bank was taken over by the present bank and nothing was being taken care of to his satisfaction. The banker did her best to mollify his concerns and, in the middle of her response, he hung up the phone. I told her that this customer was in fact rude and that she needed to pick up the phone immediately and call the next customer on the list.

I knew if she sat there and pondered what had just occurred it would fester and her confidence would wane.

As the phone gods would have it, the next person she called answered the phone and indicated that they had received the pre-approval letter and were very interested in learning more about it. This banker went from zero to hero in a matter of seconds and a broad smile crossed her face.

**Calling after hours is essential to getting in touch with your clients.**

I encourage you to set time aside to make calls after normal banking hours. Also, many banks are open on Saturdays and this is an excellent time to call your customers.

In fact, when we do our Relationship Calling™ workshops we conduct the training between the hours of 12:00 PM and 7:00 PM so that we can make contact with those clients who are unavailable during the day. Evening calling should become a part of your normal routine. You will be surprised how productive you can be in just one hour of calling after 5:00 PM. You can be totally focused on the task at hand because the phone stops ringing and branch traffic ceases.

# BUSINESS CALLING

**P**ROSPECTING AS A BUSINESS BANKER shares some of the same tenets as prospecting on the consumer side of the bank. Business Bankers are no more enthusiastic to call on businesses than Personal Bankers are about calling customers so the resistance and anxiety are equal. Also, goals are a constant for both sides. However, there are a few distinct differences: the preparation, the best time to call, the addition of the gatekeeper, and some of the objections are in fact, different.

As a business banker it is crucial that you are making targeted, quality calls. This is not a 'call anybody' process. My goal is to make you both efficient and proficient. All of the training I provide is irrelevant if bankers aren't calling people they actually want to speak with. Is everyone a prospect? Of course not! But there are plenty of qualified prospects to choose from and with a little pre-call planning you can increase your rate of success. Pre-call preparation can be a bit tedious, but the upfront work will make your calls easier and more productive.

**What information do you need to ensure that you're calling on a quality prospect?** If you are like the majority of bankers making acquisition calls, it is not your sole responsibility. Making the calling process as efficient as possible will make your entire job, not just prospecting itself, much more manageable. The first thing you need to do is gather some good information to vet the businesses you are targeting and help you create your own call list. That's right; you need to be in charge of creating quality leads for yourself. Don't rely on anyone to hand you a list. One of the common laments I hear from bankers after they have gone through our training is, "I wish I would have been better prepared." Although most banks will try to provide you with a list of "qualified prospects" it's been my experience that oftentimes these lists are not updated and the information lacks accuracy.

The bank is concerned with your goals. If you don't make your goals, you can't use the excuse that the list was rubbish. In the acclaimed screen play *Glen Garry Glen Ross* the character played by Jack Lemmon constantly decries, "If you give me the good leads I will be successful." Be in charge of your destiny and control the process by creating your own leads. Your goal is to always have a minimum of fifty quality prospects that you have personally researched and plan to contact for an appointment. Keep in mind that you do not need to research fifty names for each calling session. You're constantly adding and deleting names but your goal should be to have a list of fifty moving names to contact at any given time.

Let's look at some vital "Need-to-Knows" before you start calling:

> **Number of years in business**
> **Annual sales revenue**
> **Industry segment**
> **Number of employees**
> **Physical address and Phone Number**
> **Are they headquartered in your general marketing area?**
> **Decision Maker's Name**

All of this information will provide insight as to whether this company fits your bank's acquisition profile.

I'm always surprised when bankers come to my workshops with the name of the business and other pertinent data but lack the name of the decision maker. The decision maker's name is critical in helping you get past the gatekeeper. You cannot open the call and ask to speak to the person who handles the banking. If this is going to be your approach then don't waste your time calling. With very limited research it's very easy to learn the name of the decision maker, so do your homework and don't come across as an amateur. What if the information the bank gave me does not list the owner? Look it up or don't call.

That begs the question, who is the decision maker?   The majority of you reading this book are calling on privately held companies (mostly small businesses) with annual sales under $20mm.

For all intents and purposes the decision maker is going to be the president or owner.  In some instances it may be a CFO or controller.  Regardless, I would recommend that you always attempt to contact the owner first.  If they defer to someone else in the organization, your approach when speaking with the deferred party should always be assumptive. You can introduce yourself and the bank then say, "I just spoke with the president for the purpose of setting up a personal meeting.  She suggested I speak with you.  Would Friday at 4:00 PM work for you?"  This is what I call an implied referral.  If you're a Commercial Calling Officer calling on large corporate accounts and publicly held companies, it is not uncommon to have multiple banking relationships.  An appropriate initial contact would be the CFO or an assistant controller, depending on the size of the company.

**Where do you get quality information?** There are a number of online resources that provide excellent, up to date information on businesses so the research is done for you. Here are a few of my favorite resources that are invaluable to bankers:

**Referenceusa.com** (Accessible through the public library). You will need a library card to access this on-line.  Access is free and you can download 25 names at a time.

**Hoovers Near Here** - This is a free app available for the iPhone and iPad. It is one of the best I have seen.   It will capture your location and provide you with actionable data on companies in your marketing area. You can set selection criteria by sales size, # of employees, industry etc.

**First Research** - Provides valuable information on Industry profiles and trends.

**Linked-in** – Provides you up-to-date background and bio info on key executives.

**Company's website -** This is an excellent source of information and should be reviewed prior to your initial phone call and also before your actual face-to-face appointment.

When compiling a prospect list using outside resources, it is imperative that you scrub your list against your internal database so you don't inadvertently call a customer thinking they are a prospect or call on a prospect that another banker may already have contacted.

**Use referrals to augment your database**. Referrals are an easy way to get qualified prospects, however, most bankers fail to get them. Why? Because they don't ask and when they do ask they make their question too general. "Do you know anyone else who can use our services?" This question generally elicits a response like "no one really comes to mind," from your customer. When asking for referrals you must get specific and narrow your customer's universe. As a Banker you are privy to a wealth of information about your customer. You know their accountant's name, you know their trade references and your customer is typically familiar with other adjacent business owners. So now you need to be specific with your customer when asking for referrals. For example ask, "I have never met your accountant could you provide me with an introduction?" or "I noticed that you do a substantial amount of business with XYZ could you provide me with an introduction to the president?" By using this referral asking model you have directed your customer to a specific name and made it easy for them to assist you. Looking for opportunities within your existing customers' universe will add to you database.

**Calling an adequate number of prospects is paramount to achieving your goals.** Our data indicates that two thirds of the time when you attempt to reach the decision maker they are unavailable. So if you only call five people, three of them simply won't be there, one has moved away and the last person doesn't want to see you now – ever - never. Thus, if you don't have enough suspects to contact you're not going to be successful.

So what is an adequate number of suspects to call? Let's start with your current conversion rate. Of the number of people you reach, not just call, but also actually get a hold of, what percentage do you convert into an appointment? Let's assign a conversion rate of ten percent, which is about standard for the banking industry. Using this 10% conversion rate we need to speak with 10 decision makers to get 1 appointment.

Now we must factor in that 66% of the time the decision maker is unavailable so we need to call 30 suspects so we can reach 10 and get our 1 appointment.

Now if you want to make two new prospect appointments per day, which is an excellent goal, the number of calls now doubles to 60. This becomes a daunting task. Your conversion rate is directly related to what you say when the decision maker answers the phone. The two major mistakes most Business Bankers make when calling are that they begin selling services rather than the appointment and they give up prematurely when they encounter initial resistance from the prospect. I am confident I can help you double, if not triple, your conversion rate. Thus you will make fewer calls and get more quality appointments.

**Opening the call** Your business call will open in much the same fashion as a consumer banking call. I want you to identify yourself and the bank branch so that the prospect understands that you are working within the local community.

I also want to remind you to always ask for someone's time. For example, the opening could go something like this: *"Mr. Big my name is Jay Mann and I am with Bank of Gehegan. Did I catch you at a good time"*?

**Sell appointments not products.** Under no circumstances should you be trying to sell products when you call on a business. Unlike when you're calling on a customer from the bank and you have some information about the banking relationship; when you call on a business, you have yet to establish a relationship. If you start pushing product over the phone you're not going to generate interest and are more likely to simply turn off the decision maker. The only thing you should be selling is the appointment. Once you're in front of someone you will be able to assess their needs and present them with appropriate solutions. As I stated earlier when, you lead with a product or service, you limit your audience and set yourself up for a higher degree of resistance.

Here is an opening you can use. *"We work with many local businesses and professionals assisting them with their business banking needs. My purpose in calling today is to arrange a brief introductory meeting to discuss our commercial banking services with you. Would next Tuesday at 1:00 PM work for you?"*

If you say this instead of launching into a product push, twenty percent of the time you'll get the appointment. The other eighty percent of the time either you'll get an objection or they'll ask you, "Specifically what do you want to talk about?" This question can be a trap because you think you now must mention a product in order to satisfy their curiosity. You need to keep your response broad and general and stay focused on the appointment. For example you might say, "*We offer a wide array of business banking services, many which we can tailor to your specific needs. It is difficult to assess your needs over the phone and that is why I would like to meet with you personally.*" "*Does Tuesday afternoon at 1:00 PM work for you or would Friday morning at 8:00 AM be better?*"

By avoiding the product-push trap, you can maintain greater control over the call and remain focused on the call's objective – the appointment.

**Be specific when asking for the appointment.** It is critical that you have your appointment calendar in front of you when making calls. Never ask for an appointment by saying, "What's good for you?" This tells the prospect that you have nothing going on and you have all the time in the world. People like to do business with busy people so ask for a specific time and a specific day. Avoid asking for the appointment on the day following your call. This also implies that you are not busy. Furthermore, the chances of your prospect's calendar being full on that day are much greater. I suggest asking for the appointment 3 to 4 days out from the day you are calling. If this time is not conducive to the prospect's calendar then ask for another specific date and time. You can use an alternate choice date and time if you prefer. Remember your time is just as important as the prospect's. Don't send a subservient message.

Here are some possible responses to a few typical objections you will frequently receive from the decision maker.

**I AM HAPPY WITH MY BANK** "*That's fine. Many of the companies I speak with have a good relationship with their existing bank. It's certainly not my intent to ask you to make a banking change based on a brief meeting. If we met personally I could describe how our approach could possibly benefit you. It certainly does not hurt to explore another option. **I have some open time on Thursday at 11:30 AM or Friday at 4:00 PM. Which of those times work best for you?**"*

**TELL ME OVER THE PHONE** *"We take a total approach to addressing the financial needs of our clients. I certainly don't expect you to divulge your financial strategies over the phone and that's why I wanted to meet with you personally.* **How does next Tuesday at 3:00 PM look on you calendar?"**

**I DON'T HAVE A NEED FOR YOUR SERVICES** *"I recognize that your need may not be imminent. In fact, many of the companies I Initially meet with do not have a pressing need for our services. I am calling to arrange a brief meeting to introduce myself and provide you with an overview of our approach. In this way, should a need arise in the future, you will have an alternate resource ready to consider.* **Would Friday morning at 8:00 AM work for you?"**

Notice that upon answering the objection, we always close for the appointment. This is critical in maintaining control of the call and keeping focused on our objective – **THE APPOINTMENT**

Any response to an objection should be made in a professional tone that doesn't suggest any frustration or irritation on your part. Remember that your voice is your only connection to the decision maker and it's imperative that you maintain the highest standard of professionalism. Your conduct over the phone is the decision maker's first impression of you and is the beginning of your relationship.

The majority of objections from the decision maker should be considered reflexive and can be addressed with a short response. The only time to probe into an objection is when we need clarification; for example, the prospect states that he had a "Bad Past Experience" or that he Just Changed Banks. We need to learn a little bit more about the circumstances before we respond.

**Anticipate and manage objections.** As with any prospecting call you should prepare for objections. As we mentioned earlier, the majority of telephone objections are reflexive. They're merely an expected part of the process, which is great, because if we know they're coming, we can prepare for them with appropriate responses.

**You can't get an appointment if you can't get past the gatekeeper.**

Most people assume that the gatekeeper's job is to keep people out. This perception establishes a tension between the caller and gatekeeper. This tension then creates an adversarial relationship detrimental to success. You want the gatekeeper to be your ally, not your adversary. Your objective is to get the gatekeeper to assist you and not resist you. In fact, by merely shifting your perception of the gatekeeper's role you can impact the outcome of the call. What if the gatekeeper's job is to merely gather more information?  If this is indeed his or her role, then your job is to provide him or her with the necessary information to put you through to the decision maker. The key here is to understand the typical questions the gatekeeper is going to ask (most of which you probably know) and answer his or her question(s). A major mistake most bankers make is to provide more information than is requested.

When you give too much information, you allow the gatekeeper to make a decision on the relevance and importance of your call.

For example, let's say I open the call with the gatekeeper by saying something like this, "Hi, my name is Jay Mann and I am with Bank of Gehegan. I was calling to speak with Ms. Hill. Is she in?" I will bet that many of you are thinking that is exactly what I say. I know it is because I have heard it over a thousand times from bankers that have attended my training.  Let's analyze two key pieces of information we gave the gatekeeper in this example. First, we told him or her we were with a bank, information that was not requested by the gatekeeper. Secondly, we asked if the decision maker was in, thus implying that our call was not expected.  Now the gatekeeper has information with which to make a decision on whether or not to pass the call through. Our goal is to limit the amount of information we provide and not volunteer information that is not requested.  We should approach the gatekeeper with an attitude of expectancy and assumption.  It is easy to convey this message when you are confident.

Let's explore this attitude of expectancy.  When you have an appointment with someone at his or her place of business and you encounter the receptionist you typically say, "Hi my name is ........ And I am here to see Ms. Hill." You voice and mannerisms convey confidence and you have an attitude of expectancy.

Let's take this same attitude of expectancy and assumption and apply it to the phone.  Suppose we said, "Good morning, this is Jay Mann calling for Mr. Hill." I think you will agree that it sounds to the gatekeeper that your call is expected and you are assuming you will be put through without any further questions. **"This is...calling for..."** is a simple, straightforward and effective approach. If the gatekeeper wants more information, they will have to ask for it. If the gatekeeper poses a question, then answer the question and follow up your answer with, "Could you put me through, please?"

Getting past the gatekeeper requires a cordial, confident, expectant and assumptive attitude.

You'll increase your odds of getting to the decision maker if you answer the gatekeeper's question and request action.

This economic formula is contrary to an approach that favors making small talk and ingratiating the gatekeeper in the hope that she'll put you through based on your friendly exchange. Idle chitchat doesn't help the gatekeeper to do her job and rarely endears you to her.

Let's look at some questions that gatekeepers typically will ask and some possible responses.

If they ask for the name of your company, simply provide the name of the bank.

If they ask if the decision maker is expecting your call then answer truthfully and say, "No".

If they ask what the call is regarding, answer with, "I wanted to get his/her opinion on a couple of ideas we have on possibly improving cash flow and reducing operating expenses. Can you kindly put me through?" This response to the gatekeeper's question is effective because by asking an opinion you place yourself in a less aggressive role. In addition, the issues of cash flow and expenses are directly related to the management of the company and obviously are not something the gatekeeper could necessarily assist you with. I would urge you to avoid talking about banking when the gatekeeper asks, "What is the call about?" Primarily because we are giving the gatekeeper information with which they think they can make a decision on; which is the company's banking.

Typically gatekeepers will not be making decisions on cash flow and expenses.

Having responses at the ready to answer the gatekeeper's questions keeps you in control of the conversation. Remember your objective is to speak with the decision maker. Answer the question and make a request for action. Do these responses work a hundred percent of the time? Of course not. What we're attempting to do is to increase the percentages. If you're successful ten percent of the time and we can give you some ideas to make you successful fifteen percent of the time, we have increased your productivity by fifty percent. A return on investment I'm sure you will take.

If the decision maker is unavailable at the time of your call then ask the gatekeeper when would be the best time to call back. Once the gatekeeper provides you with a callback time say, "Great, I'll call then. Do you have his direct number?" Asking for a direct number needs to become a habit and part of your approach. Most of the time, the gatekeeper will tell you he cannot give that information to you. Remember, I said most of the time, not all of the time. Keep in mind we're playing percentages and if we get the direct number ten percent of the time it is a lot better then zero which is what you get when you don't ask. Having the direct number allows you to contact the decision maker early or late in the day when the gatekeeper is not there.

**Get the gatekeeper's name** The majority of the time the decision maker will be unavailable at the time of your call, thus necessitating multiple follow up calls. Once we have determined the best time to call back and attempted to get the prospect's direct number always ask the gatekeeper for their name. It should be phrased accordingly, "By the way what is your name?" Once they give you their name say, "Thanks (use their name) I appreciate your assistance."

Be sure to document the gatekeeper's name in your contact management system and use the gatekeeper's name in all future attempts to contact the prospect. This will enable you to develop rapport on subsequent calls. When you treat the gatekeeper as the professional she is and recognize her role as someone to assist you and not resist you, you will find gaining access to the decision maker will be a whole lot easier.

Throughout the entire calling process you must stay focused on the objective at hand and maintain clarity of purpose. When the gatekeeper answers the phone, our objective is singularly focused – to speak with the decision maker! When the decision maker answers the phone, our objective is also singularly focused – to get an appointment!

**Should I leave a message?** I would suggest not leaving a message on your initial call. Generally messages don't get returned and if the call is returned, it's frequently returned at an inopportune time. This may convey to the prospect that you're not organized.

In addition, and perhaps more significantly, it diminishes your control over the prospecting process. If your prospect is not available when you call the best strategy to employ is to ask when would be an appropriate time to call back.

If you reach voicemail the philosophy is the same, don't bother to leave a message on the initial call for the reasons I've already stated. The exception to this rule is if you were referred to this prospect or if you were following up on an email or a letter which you sent, then always leave a message. If you find that you're always getting voicemail, try mixing it up and calling at three different times during the day. If after three attempts you are confronted with voicemail again, you can leave the following message, "This Jay Mann with Bank of Gehegan. I have a couple ideas that may have a positive impact on your company. I can be reached at _____. Thanks." The brevity, simplicity and vagueness of the message will give you the greatest chance of getting a return call.

**Using email for those difficult to reach prospects can be an effective tool.** I recommend not asking for an email address on your initial conversation with the gatekeeper for two reasons: First, our goal is to speak directly with the decision maker and second, we want to build some initial rapport with the gatekeeper (getting their name).

Typically on subsequent calls they will be more willing to provide you with that information.

**Pre-approach contact.** Written communication prior to a call can provide numerous benefits if executed well. Letters or emails offer a personal touch that can be customized and organized. This approach is not to be confused with a mass mailing campaign being undertaken by the bank. Mass mailing campaigns are similar to print and media campaigns; they create awareness, not action.

You should be selective with whom you send pre-approach correspondence to. Typically, hard to reach prospects (e.g. doctors and attorneys) are good candidates. If you want to send a pre-approach e-mail, or a letter in advance of a call remember to keep the communication brief, direct, and concise. Don't be verbose and send them large, overwhelming packages of collateral to sift through. Marketing material can be less personal than a letter or e-mail.

First you want to gain their attention. Mention a strong benefit in the very first paragraph. Posing a strong opening question can be an excellent way to pull in the reader. "When was the last time your banker discussed... with you?" or "Have you considered the impact of ... on your business?" Much like a phone call you have very little time to capture your reader. Don't waste that space on lots of dull information about the history of the bank. The letter is about them, not the bank.

Next you want to generate interest. Unless your prospect is convinced that meeting with you will advance his or her business, there is little to no chance that he or she will waste their precious time with you.

Once you've generated interest you want to subtly suggest that he or she may be missing out on the benefits you can provide, "Working with an experienced banker eliminates, improves, and decreases..." The key is to choose language that motivates the recipient to act.

Finally, you want to commit to following up by saying, "I will be contacting you on...to arrange a mutually convenient time for us to meet personally and further discuss the value we can provide." By citing a specific follow up time, the onus is now on you to follow up.

The key is to follow up. Since following up on a specific date is critical, you want to limit the number of prospects you send them to. I would suggest no more than five per week. Remember it will take at least three attempts to make contact so five letters equals fifteen calls. If you send out too many, you could get overwhelmed and not follow up as you indicated you would in your correspondence and thus lose credibility. The pre-approach is just that. It's a commitment to make future contact. If you merely send out e-mails and letters in the hopes that someone will respond, you'll find that the results are extremely poor. Be selective and disciplined in your approach.

**What I if I mispronounce the prospect's name?** Sometimes we let the smallest things become an impediment to our success. I am going to let you in on a little secret. You are not the first person who has ever mispronounced your prospect's name. Countless people before you have done the same thing. People mispronounce my name quite often and I never take offense. I am pretty confident that your prospect will not take offense either.

Whenever I encounter a name that appears to be difficult to pronounce, I always take a stab at it and then ask the prospect if I am pronouncing their name correctly. If I am wrong, the prospect will give me the correct pronunciation of their name. I then write it down phonetically on my notes so I can pronounce it correctly on future calls. Again, this is a minor detail and should not serve as a reason not to call a particular prospect.

**Calling on the medical profession.** Of all the professionals, doctors are perhaps the most difficult to reach. There is usually only one reason why the doctor is in the office – to see patients. So when you call, the overwhelming majority of the time you will hear this from the receptionist, "The doctor is with a patient." As we have discussed, statistically 66% of the time the decision maker is unavailable, with doctors it is closer to 90%.

Doctors are excellent prospects and can be very profitable customers. So we must not give up on calling them just because they're so hard to reach.

My first job in sales was working for Lanier Business Products, selling dictating machines (some of you reading this book probably don't even know what a dictating machine is). Doctors were our best prospects because they had to use our product to record patient histories and physicals. Getting in front of the doctor was just as hard for me as it is for you. However, I learned to do something a little bit different when it came to calling on doctors. Doctors will typically reserve some time each week to meet with the pharmaceutical representatives. Often times it is right after lunch.

When you make your initial call to a doctor's office the opening will be the same as any other professional or business owner. You say, "This is. calling for Dr. Lovett." Typically the receptionist will say, "The doctor is with a patient; is there something I can help you with?" Your response, "Yes maybe you can."(This is where we will give information to get information). "As I mentioned my name is ……. and I am with Bank of Gehegan. Does the doctor make the decision regarding banking for the practice or is there someone else that is involved with that?"

There are three possible answers you will get when you ask this question. Here are the three responses:

A. "Yes. The doctor handles the banking for the practice."
B. "No. Our office manager handles that."
C. "No. The banking is handled by our business manager or accountant."

Here are some possible tactics for each of these scenarios.

**Yes. The doctor handles the banking for the practice.** You should respond by asking when does the doctor see detail people or pharmaceutical salespeople. If the receptionist gives you a day and time, I suggest you just show up at the doctor's office at that specific date and time. No appointment is necessary - just show up. This will enhance your chances of speaking with the doctor directly, making a brief introduction and determining a time to sit down with the doctor for a more formal presentation.

**No. Our office manager handles that.** Your objective here is to speak directly to the office manager and close them for an appointment. Keep in mind that the doctor will probably make the final decision on the banking but the office manager is your conduit in.

**No. Our business manager or accountant handles the banking.** These individuals are separate entities so we need to get their name and phone number. We can call to make an appointment with them to discuss banking alternatives.

Once you reach the business manager or accountant use the same implied referral approach. *"I recently contacted Doctor Lovett's office for the purpose of setting up an appointment to discuss our banking services. They suggested I speak with you. Do you have some open time next Friday afternoon at 3:00 PM?"*

Business managers and accountants are great contacts because once you develop a relationship with them you now open yourself up to their universe of clients which can be a bonanza for you.

Another suggestion on contacting doctors is through referrals. I'm sure that most of you have a doctor as a client. You need to leverage that relationship and ask all of your doctor clients for referrals to other physicians. This will soften the call because you can use the referral as the reason for the call.

**Should I Call to Confirm My Appointments?** My philosophy on confirming appointments goes like this; if the customer is coming into the branch to meet with you then always confirm; if you are going to meet with a prospect at their place of business never confirm. On prospect appointments I would recommend capturing their email and sending an appointment reminder via their email or electronic calendar. Also provide them with your phone number, letting them know that should anything change they can call you.

The majority of prospects will call to reschedule if they cannot keep the appointment; that is why I recommend not to confirm. If the prospect does pull a no-show, then you have a reciprocal situation and more than likely the prospect will reschedule out of courtesy. Should the prospect tell you to call to confirm, then by all means you should honor their request.

**When is the best time to call?** Not to be trite, but I like to use the Nike commercial "Just Do It." With the exception of Monday mornings, I believe that carving out thirty to forty- five minutes of prospecting time each day will ensure success. As I have mentioned several times throughout this book, the odds are against you getting through to the decision maker on the first call. They are in meetings, in the field, on the phone, on vacation etc. This is exacerbated when we call certain professionals at the wrong time. For example, calling attorneys in the morning is usually not the best time since they are on their way to or in court. I would suggest calling attorneys later in the day, perhaps after 4 or even after 5 PM.

If you're calling on a manufacturing company, calling before 8 AM is a good time since most owners arrive at their place of business before 8 AM. If you're calling on a restaurant, a good time would be between 3 and 4 PM.

Keeping track of your call times and call-to-contact ratio will help determine the best time for the various industries and professionals you are calling on. If you're calling between 10 AM and 11 AM and find that eighty percent of the decision makers are unavailable, then I would suggest you change the time. The more calls you make the more you will begin to see certain patterns emerge and you can adapt your calling time to the times you have been most successful. It comes down to this: In order to get a hold of people you need to make the calls. The consistency of your effort will positively impact your contact ratio.

**Documenting your activity** It is essential to document every contact with your customers and prospects. Effective use of your bank's customer/prospect management system will save you time and allow you to effectively prepare for subsequent calls. It is not necessary to write a comprehensive record of every customer contact however; a succinct synopsis of the call will suffice. This will allow you or anyone within the bank to see what activity has transpired and what the possible next steps will be. I would suggest that when making calls you make a few notes about the content of each call and wait until after your calling session to transfer that information into the database. If you spend time updating the database after each call you will lose momentum and negatively impact the time you have allocated to make calls.

**The Multiplying Effect** Here's a simple process that will increase your prospecting effectiveness. Upon completing your appointment make it a habit to walk into the business to the left and to the business on the right. You have now made **three** calls every time you have an appointment. I have been selling most of my adult life and I can tell you emphatically that selling is nothing more than seeing the right people, at the right time, and under the right conditions. How do you know it is the right time? You don't. That is why you must take advantage of every opportunity to make people aware of what you do.

Many bankers object to the idea of walking into a business unannounced. They may feel it is unprofessional to call on someone without an appointment. For those of you that may feel this way put your pride aside and make some cold calls (or "hot knocks" as my sales manager used to say). We need to use whatever method we can to reach out to potential clients and make them aware of what we do.

Cold calling is an excellent way to learn about the businesses in your marketing area. I will guarantee you that if you adopt this discipline on every call you will find new business.

Today our prospecting efforts are limited to using the telephone since our market covers a wide geographic area both domestically and internationally. However, when I sold office products I did a lot of face-to-face cold calling. Some of my largest sales were initiated by just walking into a large law firm or commercial business unannounced. I do not tell you this to impress you but to impress upon you that the business is out there and you need to take advantage of the moment. Create your own opportunities.

**Confidence helps you succeed.** When I am conducting my workshops, participants often say they are uncomfortable in making calls and lack confidence. There is a direct correlation between confidence and success. When we are successful at any task or skill, we automatically become confident in our ability to repeat that success. Our lack of confidence on the phone is usually a result of not being successful. Success is rarely achieved by repetition alone. Success is achieved by applying proper technique over and over. If you follow the simple principles set forth in this book and apply them on a consistent basis, I guarantee you will experience a greater degree of success and your confidence will blossom accordingly.

**Staying Motivated** There is an old saying "Some days the cherries and some days the pits." Sales is a lot like life in general. We all deal with setbacks and uncertainties throughout our lives. How we react to them determines our success or failure in the future. I've talked about handling objections on the phone and dealing with the explosive "NO" that derails so many salespeople. However, there is a NO that is much more damaging and will ultimately undermine not only your calling effort, but your overall attitude. That NO is self-doubt. There will be days when your calling efforts will yield zero results. And there will be days where you have put in a lot of energy and time into a deal and end up losing it.

It is on these days that you must accept the outcome as part of the process and quickly move forward.

There have been numerous times in my selling career that I have suffered setbacks. In fact, I have been turned down many more times than I have ever been successful.

I remember a time when I first started selling. I was cold calling an office building in Santa Monica, California and I was physically escorted out of the building by the security guard and told that I was not allowed to solicit. Here I was standing outside this building totally humiliated and thinking to myself, do I really want to do this? I got into my car and drove back to the office. Looking somewhat downtrodden I encountered my boss and he asked me how I was doing. I told him I just got thrown out of an office building. He then said, "Well what did you do?" I told him I decided to come back to the office and he said, "You did the wrong thing." He said, "You should have walked across the street and gone into another building. The whole time you were driving back to the office you were thinking about your bad experience, allowing it to feed on itself when you should have let it go and kept on prospecting." I learned so much from that experience and my boss's guidance that whenever I encounter setbacks and negativity I quickly move on and do not allow it to occupy my thought process.

If you allow self- doubt to occupy your thinking you will sabotage your future efforts. If you approach each call with a positive attitude you will remain optimistic on every call. I believe we are what we think about. In his book, *As A Man Thinketh*, James Allen writes, **"All a man achieves and all that he fails is a direct result of his own thoughts."**

# MANAGING THE PROCESS

**A**LL TRAINING, AND I DO mean all training, is as good as the support and execution that occurs post-training. While micromanagement is not advocated in most areas of leadership, when it comes to sales leadership and specifically to prospecting it is mandatory. If you don't inspect what you expect, then you get no respect. Training is not a silver bullet. Olympic athletes don't get coached for a single day. They're coached, and challenged, and supported every day to achieve excellence.

In order to achieve the highest results you need to be dialed into sales activity weekly. If you're merely checking sales numbers once a month, then it's difficult (if not impossible) to assess and address specific challenges that are compromising performance. By the time you try to solve the problem you're two months out, and your evaluation and solution to any problem is merely guessing.

There isn't a bank in the country that doesn't know how many checking accounts they opened each day of the month. It's basic tracking. The same attention needs to be paid to each banker's outbound calling activity.

You can't simply hand a banker a phone and a call list and expect magic. That's an absurd expectation destined for failure.

A phone and a call list are tools, but without skills they don't produce results. Could you build a house with just the materials?

Trial and error is an expensive substitute for training. Not only does a lack of training perpetuate bad habits leading to bad results and low morale, it also wastes valuable opportunities. It is a vicious cycle. Institutions pay a high price for electing not to train their bankers. The truth is the cost is incalculable, because we can't measure lost revenue from lack of engagement, we can only speculate.

If your bankers aren't successful, it's a reflection on a lack of training and leadership. I've managed numerous sales teams in my career and I can tell you that at the end of the day I was responsible for whether or not my sales people made their goals. That was my job.

As a sales manager my goal was to make my sales people better. If I didn't make them better they weren't going to make money and they would quit. Turnover in sales is a cancer that eats away at morale and profitability. It is very costly to interview, hire, and train salespeople. If my salespeople were successful they would make my job easier because they would stay and turn-over would be mitigated. I believed that training people was critical to their success and the success of the organization. Being a good manager meant getting in the trenches and doing all the things I asked my salespeople to do. If you do what you ask others to do you'll gain their respect. Furthermore, you'll develop a motivated team that wants to succeed.

**Proof is in the pudding.** At the beginning of our workshops, we always ask the participants to report their conversion rates. In other words, of the times you actually reach the decision maker, what percentage of the time do you make an appointment? The average response is 10% in any group and frequently the answer may be 5% or below. Understanding that these numbers are offered by the participants themselves --- and are very likely naturally inflated--- gives you a fairly dismal report of the overall success rate of prospecting. No wonder people hate making calls.

However, after a day of training, just one day, we are able to-increase those dismal conversion rates up anywhere from 30% – 40%. I bring this to your attention so that you're better able to understand the magnitude of training and post-training support. Anyone who is willing can learn to do this. The level of experience and product knowledge has little to nothing to do with whether or not a banker can set an appointment with a customer. The determining factor is whether they have been trained.

In order to sustain growth, and develop a habit of calling that will be integrated into the daily schedule, it's imperative to take care to oversee and support the training once it's done. While officers of the bank are excited and motivated after training, once they return to the bank, they can easily succumb to all of the distractions of daily business and lose sight of calling. Post training performance can be maximized through what I call the "A, B, C's" of management: **Accountability, Behavior, and Consistency**.

# ACCOUNTABILITY

In setting goals it is imperative to be realistic. When you set expectations too high it can have an adverse affect on morale. Unrealistic goals frustrate rather than motivate. Most bankers will have numerous responsibilities other then business development. For example a Branch Manager is responsible for the administration and profitability of their branch. A Relationship Manager typically has portfolio responsibility, which involves maintaining the profitability of their book of business. A Personal Banker must handle incoming customers and open new accounts. So what is a reasonable goal?

I believe that a reachable and meaningful goal for any banker that is not solely dedicated to business development should be 4 – 5 appointments per week with NEW prospects. This number should double for those officers whose sole responsibility is new business acquisition. Let's look at the math of 4 prospect appointments per week -16 per month - 192 per year.
If the officer was able to close 20% of those prospects, that would mean 38 new relationships per year. I think from a performance standpoint that would be an excellent year. As I mentioned, appointment goals will vary based on each banker's overall job description but keep the goals reasonable.

Tracking performance is a crucial component of accountability as well. Some of my clients just track the number of appointments. However, this will provide you with a very limited picture of each banker's calling effectiveness. I recommend that each manager track the number of **calls, contacts,** and **appointments** that are made by a given banker in order to turn prospecting into a meaningful, result driven activity. It is also advisable to have the banker note the time of day they are making their calls. This information will allow a manager to assess conversion rates, determine if the calling times are appropriate and assess whether the banker is working with a quality list. All of this information helps to manage the activity, steward success, and reduce the frustration that may cause a banker to avoid calling.

Each one of these components provides valuable information about the process. You can't simply measure the number of appointments, because it tells you nothing about a banker's activity ratios. It may have taken a hundred contacts to get two appointments, which means there's a gap in training. When you track these three components certain patterns will emerge and allow you to coach to both strengths and weaknesses.

Asking your bankers to track this data should not be seen as a policing method. It should be viewed as a positive approach to gauging one's performance.

A one-on-one weekly debrief to review the tracked information will provide the necessary feedback on this activity and will allow you to both coach and congratulate bankers on their efforts. Often general meetings don't have time to address the specifics of calling. A focused one-on-one meeting is time well spent to achieving optimum results. Let's take a look at an activity summary for three different bankers:

| | CALLS | CONTACTS | APPOINTMENTS |
|---|---|---|---|
| BANKER 1 | 72 | 8 | 4 |
| BANKER 2 | 72 | 24 | 2 |
| BANKER 3 | 72 | 40 | 12 |

For demonstration purposes let assume that the calling activity for each banker was the same – 72 calls. It is now very easy to have a discussion with each of these bankers regarding the outcome of their activity.

**Banker # 1** was able to achieve a 50% appointment to contact ratio, however the call-to-contact ratio was low. When the call-to-contact ratio falls below 20% it can be attributed to the following: they may be calling at the wrong time, the list they are working with is not accurate, or they may be having difficulty getting past the gatekeeper.

**Banker # 2** was able to achieve a good call-to-contact ratio. However, the contact-to-appointment ratio was low. When the contact-to-appointment ratio falls below 10% it can be attributed to the banker attempting to sell over the phone rather than selling the appointment, or they may be giving up too prematurely when they encounter resistance from the prospect.

**Banker # 3** has ideal ratios and this is what your entire team should be striving to accomplish.  Banker # 3 needs to share her best practices with the rest of the team.

As you can see from this simple tracking method, you can now sit down with your bankers on a one-on-one basis and discuss how to improve their activity ratios.

# BEHAVIOR

In order to sustain what's been learned, it's important that all of the training is reinforced internally. Remaining within the confines of the call structure we've provided will achieve higher returns. Constructive role-playing will help to familiarize people with the content and make the dialogue conversational and second nature. With enough practice these calls will be a natural extension of the banker. It's important to listen to calls and provide positive input that will help someone be more successful.

Coaching should be nurturing and not critical. Harsh judgment doesn't produce the highest result. If you want to create engaged bankers who actually don't mind calling, then set them up for success. You have to create a safe environment where people feel supported and encouraged. If you want behavior to change, acknowledge when your bankers are doing things right. Anyone can comment on when someone is doing something wrong, but it's much better to save that coaching and conversation for constructive feedback during your one-on-one meeting. Pay attention to all of the correct behavior and that behavior will multiply because people feel good about their performance.

Coaching is not just about observing; it is about doing what you ask others to do. The best form of leadership is by example. As a manager you should make calls in the presence of your bankers.

Many mangers want to manage by telling and not by doing. Sometimes mangers think that because they are a manager they don't need to pick up the phone. Well I have news for you, they are wrong. As I mentioned previously when I was learning how to sell I had a number of excellent mentors. My regional manager and my direct supervisor would always do what they asked me to do. Whether it was picking up the phone to make an appointment or making a face-to-face cold call, they would always step up to the plate and make the calls with me.

I learned so much from this type of training and leadership. Not only were they telling me what to do; they also put themselves on the spot and showed me how to do it. As a manager you will gain respect by doing what you ask others to do.  Lead by example and you will develop a dedicated and motivated team.

Posting outcomes is an excellent way to motivate people to achieve higher results, but it's important that you recognize those achievements. Recognition can be more effective than money in expressing appreciation. When you value and acknowledge your bankers, you'll inspire them to perform at their very best.  Success breeds success.  Emails from senior management acknowledging a job well done also provides motivation.

Just for the record, you should never make calling punitive. If someone doesn't make his or her goals, punishment is not a tool to inspire motivation. Don't keep your staff after hours, away from their families, in order to make the goals they missed. That will only breed low self-esteem and resentment; neither of which contributes to a successful salesperson.  Shame and punishment are the tools of a very poor manager.

# CONSISTENCY

If you want to learn to play golf, lessons are only the first step. It's constant, proper practice that improves your game. This is also true with calling. Managers should provide each banker with uninterrupted, scheduled time to make these calls for forty-five minutes per day off the platform.

If you want bankers to be successful, then you need to create an environment for them to succeed. Asking anyone to make calls on the fly is a losing strategy that will fall apart quickly and produce negative results. No one can reasonably make calls with constant interruptions from co-workers and customers.   The parade of interruptions is not conducive to the focus required to make appointments on the phone.

Create space that allows for uninterrupted calling and teach your staff not to disturb someone who is prospecting. If you provide for protected call time you elevate its importance and everyone starts to respect the process, thereby creating greater success.

You may try to argue that there are times when it's necessary to interrupt someone, but the truth is there are many times during the day that a banker is unable to answer the phone or meet with a customer who walks into the bank unannounced. Typically, someone else can assist that customer. In the case of inbound calls, messages can be left and bankers can follow up after their prospecting activity.

If you allow prospecting to become an afterthought, you diminish its importance and foster a reactive culture that's too scattered to control, which leads to poor results.  If you are going to allow bankers to make calls sporadically throughout the day then you are setting them up for failure. Keep in mind the most difficult call to make is the first one.  When calls are scattered throughout the day each call becomes a first call. I like to make the analogy of a golfer going to the driving range and asking for one ball and then returning in an hour to hit one more.  I don't think they would see much of an improvement in their game.

One of the reasons we get such success during the live calling portion of our training is that we have uninterrupted time. The dramatic increase in conversion rates is absolutely extension of training, but it also speaks to creating an environment for success rather than stress. Nothing replaces focused time.

For Business Bankers I recommend weekly calling blitzes to sustain activity and maintain momentum. I have had clients gather their bankers together by region and make calls for a two-hour period every Thursday. Other clients due to logistics have their bankers participate in a conference call prior to their blitz time and then report their results on a follow up conference call after the blitz. .

I strongly suggest that evening calling become a routine part of customer calling. As I stated before, when we do our Relationship Calling™ we conduct the training between the hours of 12:00 PM and 7:00 PM so that we can make contact with those clients who are unavailable during normal business hours.

Regardless of how you design your group calling effort, participation should be mandatory and it must be conducted on a regular schedule. It is management's job to make it fun by providing an enthusiastic atmosphere. You can offer a gift card or movie tickets to the person who makes the most appointments, thus adding a competitive edge. The overall value of this activity is that the calls are getting done. **No excuses**.

# CONCLUSION

The information in this book is a distillation of more than 30 years of data and experience. I wanted to deliver this information in the most accessible and economical form so that any banker who has responsibility for deepening relationships with their customers or acquiring new customers would have everything they need to be successful. We have discussed certain strategies to employ when making calls. But just as important, we have made it a point to dispel some myths about selling and hopefully change your attitude about making calls. As we have stated in the book "Nothing works 100% of the time". However, if you are successful getting appointments 10% of the time and we have given you some ideas to make you successful 15% of the time, this is a return on investment you will gladly take. Use this book as a resource and professional development tool.

Your bank hired you because you're capable, smart and competent. You now have everything you need to increase profitability, enhance your career and become a top performer. Your capacity to develop relationships in business will serve you well now and in the future. It is a skill that you can continue to nurture and belongs to you. And it is a skill that will always be in demand. The difference between success and status quo is commitment to the work. Success at any activity begins with desire and is accomplished through discipline. Discipline is the one common thread through which results are achieved and maintained. Without the discipline to do this activity on a regular and consistent basis I guarantee that your performance will not improve. If we do not exercise on a regular basis our muscles begin to atrophy. The same is true for your prospecting activity. It is essential to maintain a full pipeline of prospects at all times. I have never met a salesperson that says, "I am getting out of selling because I have too many prospects." The primary reason salespeople fail is that they suffer from a dearth of prospects.

Here is Gehegan's Law: **THE FEWER PROSPECTS YOU HAVE, THE GREATER PRESSURE YOU PUT ON YOURSELF AND YOUR PROSPECT. THE MORE PROSPECTS YOU HAVE, THE LESS PRESSURE YOU PUT ON YOURSELF AND YOUR PROSPECT.**

Do yourself, your customers and prospects a favor. Pick up the phone now and start opening relationships with your clients and prospects.

Congratulations! You are now on the next stage of your professional journey. I wish you much success!

# ABOUT THE AUTHOR

J OHN J. GEHEGAN IS PRESIDENT of Gehegan & Associates, a San Diego, California based sales training firm, established in 1983. He is a graduate of Iona College and possesses a BBA with a major in Marketing. Gehegan & Associates provides telephone sales skills training programs to the financial services industry.

Mr. Gehegan brings real world experience as a successful salesperson and a sales manager, into his training programs and relates his background to the challenges faced by bankers who take a proactive approach to business development.

Mr. Gehegan has developed a solid reputation within the financial services industry for his results oriented training programs, geared for both retail and commercial calling officers. Tens of thousands of bankers across the country and internationally have attended the Business Development Workshop and the Relationship Calling™ Workshop to increase their confidence and effectiveness using the telephone to set appointments with prospective and existing customers.

Mr. Gehegan has conducted his workshops for financial institutions and sales organizations throughout the United States, Canada, Puerto Rico, Australia, New Zealand, Singapore, Hong Kong, Philippines, Taiwan and the United Arab Emirates.

Clients have included major money center banks, regional banks and community banks.

Additional information regarding our training along with a client list can be found at **gehegan.com**